MW00941841

WORDS FOR LIPS TOO BUSY KISSING

Cynthia Gomez
@Human_Writes

WORDS FOR LIPS TOO BUSY KISSING

Copyright © 2016 by Cynthia Gomez

All rights reserved. Printed in the United States of America. No part of this book may be used or reproduced in any manner whatsoever without prior written consent except in the case of brief quotations embodied in critical articles and reviews.

The scanning, uploading and distribution of this or any part of this book via the Internet or via any other means without the permission of the publisher is illegal and punishable by law. Please purchase only authorized electronic editions and do not participate in or encourage electronic piracy of copyrighted materials. Your support of the author's rights is appreciated.

For information, please contact

humanwritespoetry@gmail.com

Published by Cynthia Gomez

ISBN 978-1-365-05208-8

This book is one big confession. A neat drawer for the extensive mess in my head. An attempt to contain the explosion in my chest. It is every word I have ever left unsaid in fear of actually being heard. The love letter that I never sent. The ending that I never wrote. A heartfelt apology to the ones I never meant to hurt. It is every kiss I couldn't give and every last embrace I never thought I'd always miss.

And love
rattled her bones,
searching for beauty
unaware of its own.

She comes and goes,

    she ebbs and flows

    in waves that never crest.

Lest I bend her sail

    with my own breath,

    in rising storms

    she'll find her rest.

If ever there was a flower
that blossomed *inward,*
it is you.

But if only
you knew
what grave
injustice
you do
to humanity
simply
by keeping
your beauty
sheltered
from
view.

I walked into a stranger the other day
to see the place. I fit so snug inside
her space, beneath her leaky roof; empty
drawers full of people gone too soon.
Inked up walls would read to me until
I knew: Her crooked smile I'd never leave,
in fear that someone else could ever fill
that vacancy in you.

//Open House//

But she wasn't the same-
she had a *tempestuous storm* for
a heart that's only known rain
and the promise of a sunnier
morrow that never once came.

To dream you up
in peaceful shores
cannot compare to
slaying fears with you
in times of war; so
take my outstretched
hand as we endure
these daunting seas
that lie before.

There is no need
for brick or stone
to shelter thee-
when I've built
a home in you
and you in me.

My lips are laced with silent kill

to make you come alive

against your will.

"I want to consume your mind,"

she said to me-

and I didn't mind

at all the abuse;

I knew I

could use

her reckless

love excuse

to fall apart.

For what can ever come

from such implosion of the heart,

if not the most erotic of the arts?

We are such
impressionable
creatures with
liquefied hearts
we instinctively
pour into shapeless
containers to give
them their form.

//Plasticity//

Most people that like you,
like you because you come
very close to what they are
looking for in a person. But
every once in a while if you
are lucky, you come across
someone who isn't trying to
find a perfect person.
Instead, they prefer to work
through your flaws with you
because they value your
individuality more than
their own expectations.

We are
the most breathtaking
stained glass mural
you have ever
laid eyes on,

Broken up into
infinitesimal pieces
and scattered all about
our insecurities.

I hope
you don't mind,
I put my own strain of
cocaine in our last kiss.
It will glaze your tongue
with my intoxicating bliss
so your palate can never
taste of anything again
without the lingering
flavor of my name
seeping straight
into your
veins.

I'm becoming
better friends
with time;
we've talked
it through
and
understood
what's his,
was never mine.

I am passion ignited,

atoms colliding,

the gravitational tilt

of your world off its axis,

emotions divided,

sensors excited,

sex in the flesh,

love unrequited,

the thrill of an addict

filling a void

that's only expanding,

an assorted bouquet

of collective madness,

waiting for someone

to wrangle my chaos,

and *love me*

out of this sadness.

And you;

you are *toxic*, my love.

A dangerous delicacy

that tastes of desire

yet fills with regret.

The product of a world

collecting a debt that

never belonged to you.

You overcome adversity

at the expense of your innocence;

you are lifted with wisdom

but weighed down by experience;

your passions are stifled

by fear of commitment

and subsequent loss-

that's just how

you've been conditioned.

To trade in your happiness

for a little less sorrow,

to *feel less* tomorrow

and so you protect;

your kindness forever hardened

by the pangs of betrayal,

you are love hypothetical,

you are a love that's gone stale.

All the while
I slaved and toiled
to keep our dying
love in bloom,
I hadn't seen
that right behind
your browning leaves,
a new love
would sprout soon.

And I told her to
find me, at her worst.
I don't want her
iridescent smiles,
anyone will take that.

I will wait for her
salt-brimmed eyes,
paling skin and
shipwrecked frame.

When the loneliness
starts to cave in
and her knees crumble
beneath her own existence,
I will be all that remains.

Pretty girl with the half empty bottle of truth and the insatiable youth, I'm talking to you. There's more bad people out there than we care to know and all the good ones have already gone home for the night. So do me a favor and do yourself right before it gets worse. Just lay your head down, I'll tuck you in tight and turn off the stars who are stealing your light, *you are your own bright* in a world overcome by shadows, so jealous of you.

//Growing Up Too Soon//

I

am

a

butterfly

on

a

string.

To protect me

from the span of my wings

and the illicit freedom they bring.

She was an island
all on her own,
the last unturned stone
they all overlooked.
As she drifted to sleep,
the universe took turns
to unravel her dreams.

The night watched over her
with a sky full of eyes
and the shifting tides
came rolling in
to hug her shore.

Even the planets
got on their knees
to propose
with their rings,
but her loneliness
always loved her more.

And I felt like I opened my eyes
one morning inside the wrong story.
Transitions are blurry
from things I'd rather not know
like "what keeps me here,"
and "where did she go?"
A note:
She's gone to be found;
she'll come back around
at the sound of my voice
reciting *those three words*
I had long left for dead.
My dear,
I have no promises left
and neither do you.
So come back to sleep
and into this peace
that it brings,
knowing we can always rely
on the *impermanence* of things.

To this day,
I'm not
quite sure
if you truly
watered
my soul,
or if
you were
just my
rainy days.

And as your name
rolled off my tongue,
I rolled it up
and smoked it blue,
the slowest fire
to ever burn,
in silent thoughts
that scream for you.

She wore that
ravenous gaze
and filthy smile
that she knows
ignites me.
She cradled the
feverish cigarette
between her scalding lips
and sucked the pleasure dry.
How can I resist?
For there is no art
expressed more beautifully
than a woman in her most
primitive, carnal nature.

//There's nicotine in her hips//

TWISTED ROOTS

The richest soil
        cannot sustain
        a fickle tree
        afraid to root.
Yet,
        a subtle taste
        of your desire-
        and I come alive
        in desert fields.

I wanted to
stretch myself
around her to
catch the jagged
pieces of falling
sky before they
landed beneath
her feet so she
never has to look
down at the
stars. . .

What good is a rain

that waters in vain

the bountiful grain

of tomorrow,

when we are still

reaping the sorrow

of yesterday's pain?

//Droughts that smell of rain//

There are claw marks
on the inside of my skin
from wearing myself inside out.
This is where I've been staying
the last couple of nights...
But I've lost my way out from within,
all the lights have been dimmed,
their colorful hues,
and the floorboards
are coming unglued
so
I
fall.
But not into you.
Just into a smaller
and smaller
yet chaos
that we always knew
would come true.

There are no wings out there
for the broken to fly.
For what makes them broken,
is they've lost all desire to try.

I will introduce myself
to your demons
by name.

Somewhere between
a fistful of hair
and a mouthful of me,
you blurted out
"You're perfect for me."
I remember the certainty
in your voice, tasting
the thirst on your lips,
the desire in your kiss
so vividly that no matter
how furiously you try to
resist, I don't believe
for a single second
that you would taste
any differently
this time around.

Watch
for those
that promise
elaborate
castles
when they
haven't even
laid the
first brick.

Would you trade
a light that's bound to fade,
for a darkness that has always
stayed?

We are masters of silence,
yet slaves to those words
we choose to keep quiet.
Creatures with juxtaposed
features to never reveal
how *real* we can feel
beneath our own skin.
When did we forget
that the only regrets
we collect are the emotions
we're afraid to own up to?
Tell me the world makes more sense
when it reflects off my eyes,
and my eyes will only see you.
Tell me I'm not even a speck of debris
from the wreckage we made of ourselves,
and I'll dance on the ashes
of all that we knew.
Tell me it's complicated,
that it's much too soon

to feel this much again
and we should have waited-
I'd rather the slow ache of
listening to my heart break in two,
than this unspeakable silence
I keep hearing from you.

//The loud effects of a quiet mind//

Sometimes I wish

you'd stop in on your way.

These words are too rare

to not say

to an audience.

And what better

audience to choose . . . . . .

. . . than their very own muse?

One of the hardest things
I've ever had to do
was define myself,
in terms of you.
To find myself
and my own truth
in a world that's
come alive
because of you,
and not confuse the two.
To know that I am
every bit of me
in every piece of you.

//I could use a little
  more definition tonight//

I exist in a different
state of matter than you
do right now. I am a liquid
ready to take on your shape
and you are a gas ready to
dissipate into the
intimate
space
between
who
we
are
and
who
we
became.

//Love is neither created nor destroyed,
it is only experienced in the wrong form//

Clothe me in your afternoons,
I want to feel the day on you.
The way it bends its straight-ward rays,
around the ways your figure moves.

I want to slip between your sheets
and secretly undress your floral skin.
I want to see temptation break you
to unveil the artistry eclipsed within.

I want an existential love affair
with a touch of mortal sin,
until I no longer am aware
of where you end and I begin.

I'm sorry
but my heart
is temporarily
closed
for renovations.
We are
knocking down
every room to
make more room
for *only you.*

There are those

that create

and

there are those

that appreciate.

Both

are artists

in their own way.

Look for the quiet ones with the quiet eyes.

Those are the ones that carry a storm inside.

Silent observers of time,

they are born with a heart

that pours, for all humankind;

and a *beautifully twisted* kind of mind

that will find themselves a lover to skin alive,

as a testament to the voracious love

that ravages their blood.

They will siphon every doubt

out of every breath

you have yet to breathe,

and dump all your wilting organs

on the side of the road to

fill you back up to the brim

with *way more love*

than this selfish excuse of a world

could ever, *never* give.

You lay there like
undeveloped film
in the darkness of
my room, completely
exposed; and all I
could think was,
no lens could ever
capture your beauty,
and no prose could ever
unravel your soul.

Being wiser than most should
not elevate you above them.
It should give you more of
a reason to walk *among* them,
for knowledge receives praise,
but wisdom gladly gives it away.

It was always *real.*

But I was looking to *feel.*

And you were looking to *heal.*

Note To My Lover:

Yes, I am a lover
of many things and
everyone and
every *thing*.
My soul grows sick with an
overabundance of expression
I need to release through
creative affection.
How cruel is it to
witness beauty
in the flesh-
to be *moved by it*
and not celebrate it as
the masterpiece that it is?

I know you think that makes me
inconsistent
and I know how much that
terrifies you.
But don't for a second think
you would ever have to compete
with any of those fleeting faces.
There's a more permanent place
I save for you
where you can plant your feet
and never have to move.
The longer you stay there with me,
the more you will begin to replace
all of the excess in me
that is just taking up space
until all I have left,
is all that I need,
is all that is you.

Even on the
sunniest days,
you looked at me
the way a child
looks outside a
stormy windowpane;
longing to go out
and play but opting
instead to stay inside,
on the off-chance that
even the bluest of skies
could bring forth rain.

//Irrational fears we collect
  through the years//

You know you
were never meant
for any kind of
ordinary love,
so why do you
insist on trying
to find it in
ordinary places?

There are
many ways
to walk away.
Just because
they are
physically
still there,
doesn't mean
they stayed.

Maybe that's what love is-
an embellished fantasy
one creates on their own,
product of a flourishing
imagination, to which
reality can never own up to...

//Pillow talk and pipe dreams//

The taste
of a love
gone
too soon
is the
loneliest
flavor of
solitude.

Dismantle the sky
and hang up
the clouds to dry;
pour away
the buckets of rain
and sweep up the pain
you left behind when
you walked away.

Didn't your mother
ever teach you to
clean up after yourself
after you've made a mess
of someone else's world?

How is it that the more I
try to forget you, the more
it feels like the entire world
is a distraction, *from you?*

//Nowhere To Turn//

Trying to love you again
is like going back to your
childhood playground as an
adult. It's coming to terms
with the reality that the
same place you used to slay
dragons and ward off legions
of invaders is nothing more
than a few rusty pipes and
poorly scattered mulch. It
is the sad truth of seeing
things for the very first time,
as they *always* were.

I said, "sometimes I can't sleep at night
because I can't stop thinking about you."

She said, "I sleep very well at night,
because you can't stop thinking about me."

I only
keep you alive
in my poetry
because you
no longer live
in my head
and I don't
have the heart
to kill you
completely.

//Eulogy//

I've come to the conclusion
that broken people
like to be broken.
They wake up
every morning and slip
into their brokenness
like clothing. Maybe;
they've forgotten
what they look like
put together, or maybe
feeling whole has never
felt more lonely. . .

There is
no silence
more
deafening,
than that
of a heart
not beating
for you.

//White Noise//

I met a stranger at a bar,

she said she had no name;

just a strong desire

to float a while

between the particles

of rain. A thirst

for nothing more

than emptiness

to fill the empty space;

a silent yearning to exist

in a non-existent place

where she can find

where she belongs,

in a different

kind of same.

//Day drinking

our nights away//

I
like
my
coffee
black
and
my
kisses
poetic.

I wouldn't touch you,
just shamelessly
undress you
over and over
again in my head
until the temptation
breaks you . . .

And I will wear

    the color

        of your lips

           on mine,

               because

        you've

      never looked

better on me.

I can no longer
find a reason
to leave these
four walls,
for I have
discovered
the entire
world
in the
topography
of a woman.

You have this refreshing
simplicity about you.
This lighthearted sort of
righteousness in its
purest form that is unique
only to your own soul.

You have a voice that
resonates within you with
such profound sophistication.
To those that stop and listen,
it is a thing of beauty
and encouragement.

You have a light in you
that no matter how much
external forces
try to extinguish it,
it will always have
just enough spark left
to ignite the most
colossal flame.

You wake up
different
parts of me
that I didn't
even know
were asleep.

To notice when
her oldest wrinkle
wakes up a little
deeper one morning
than it did
the night before;
that's how you
thoroughly
love a woman.

//Details//

Let me
play
your body
like an
instrument
and I will
turn your
tragedy
into a
symphony.

Baby,
let's run away
to a familiar
strange place
where everyone
knows our story
and no one
knows our name.

I want you

to complete me,

but *not completely.*

I want you

to be what I need,

but I don't want

to need you.

Take me in to

set me free,

and only then

can you have

all of what

is left of me.

And it's amazing
how you can feel
a little more
put together
when the
brokenness
is shared

. . .

I want to experience
the death of a color
just so I can
watch it bleed.
I want to feel it
saturate my blanching skin,
filling in every shade
of emptiness with it's
psychedelic melanin.
I want to hear it's
polychromatic scream
within the darkest
corners of my memories.
I want to taste it's
rich undertones,
every single subtle note
against my palate's
monotone simplicity;

because maybe, if I can
understand the beauty in
death, I can understand
the beauty in me.

//Color me in//

I have lived
a thousand lives
for every death
I've died
before my time.

//The only way to cheat
 death is to live//

I wear my scars
like medals
across my chest
to remind myself that
the hemorrhaging effects
of a wounded heart
are superficial at best;
that *bleeding out-*
is just part of the process.
It's our body's way
of draining out
all of the excess,
for to grieve is an art
where we must
acknowledge the pain
before the healing can start.

//It always hurts more
before it hurts less//

I was told that dreams no longer
come true for people like us.
That the early bus has already left
and the late one has a wait
longer than the list of heartbreaks
we've picked up along the way.
That no one is willing to give up
their seat to a pair of chronic
cold feet with no discernible heartbeat.
And although the road to a good night's
sleep is just up the street,
the roads are dimly lit
and stray nightmares
lurk through the dusk
in search of stargazers like us,
who've lost sight of their stars.

//Too late always comes too soon for us//

There is an uncomfortable
peace in being a writer.
We make ourselves
vulnerable in hopes that others
can find strength in the way
we expose our naked souls-
so that even in solitude,
you are not alone.

One day
you will wake up
and your body
will feel much heavier
than ever before.
There will be anchors
on your feet and a storm
approaching your shoreline.
Time will no longer be kind to you;
every passing day will contain
a lifetime's worth of heartache
and everything you've ever known
to be true will *have left with her,*
when she left you.

//So much to undo//

Even on the good nights,

there's at least

a fragment

of a second

stretched out for

the longest of minutes

where I am empty inside.

You are
over-thinking
and
under-drinking
much too much
to be a poet.

//Think less,
  drink more//

What if I stole a kiss
from those supple
lips of yours?
I can't deny that
I've been eyeing them
in ways most people
would not approve of,
but the way your eyes
violate mine tells me
you wouldn't mind
making some time
for a little regret...

I will bend for you,
but not enough
to break.
Don't mistake
how much I'm
willing to give,
for how much I'm
willing to take.

We are two
polar opposites
caught in
each other's
magnetic fields.

Every now and again,

I invite her back into the

quiet corners of my brain,

where we can pretend

we didn't just watch ourselves

combust into flames

while we sipped our

morning coffee, *unfazed;*

and watched as the rain

put us out-

like a fading memory we keep

pressed against our chest,

for the love of the pain.

We are not lovers,

just band-aids

to each other's

festering wounds

long enough to cover

the oozing solitude

until we can find a way

to make ourselves

whole again.

Why did it take us
so long to realize
that we were never
living a lie,
your truth was just
different from mine.

I swallow the same promise
you made to me every night
like a sleeping pill
that I prescribed myself.
Chase it down with a bottle
of top shelf scotch and watch
the sun rise once again
for everyone else.
No need to concern yourself
with my health though,
everyone knows it's very hard
to overdose on a placebo.

//Habits that create addicts//

We were stuck in
temporary forevers
like a backwards memory,
reminding us
of what we had
before it ever came to be.
We loved in alternate realities,
in the in-betweens
of what it means
to speak fleeting promises
we were never meant to keep.
Living, breathing contradictions
to our own philosophies,
liberated by our own addictions
and shackled by our sovereignty.
Yet we cling with white knuckles
to the slightest possibility
that even loneliness
deserves a little company.

I will continue
to give freely
to the ones
that have only
taken from me.
If only we'd choose
to look with our hearts
instead of our eyes,
we would come to realize
they simply needed that love
much more than we ever did.

//When you don't know how to ask//

You want forever
from me,
but I can't feel
that far ahead.
So instead,
I will promise you
every tomorrow.
from today until then.

//Forever is just
  a few days away//

I woke to your face
idle in sleep,
poised on my pillow
and drenched in gold.
The day trickled down
on the slope of your lips,
unearthing the portrait
of a story untold.
Sedated you wait
for this latent blossom
to raise her colorful wings
in sovereign flight;
so in the flurry of promise
I hurry to gather,
that which I seek
before the swallow of night.
This is the mold for
that love which they speak,
but her perfect form
none seem to fit.
Probing nature's
sweet abode I cease,
before all her splendors,
for one is surely it.

I thought I felt it

in the dance of the ocean,

but defiant and restless,

it was too hard to contain.

I thought I heard it

in a nightingale's ballad,

but the first light of dawn

chased it away.

I thought I savored it

in the highest hanging fruit,

but they weren't as ripe

as they let on to be.

I thought I smelled it

in the firstborn of spring,

but as quick as it came,

it closed up to me.

I thought I saw it against

the horizon's ruby blush,

but the closer I'd get,

the more it would flee.

Then I pried my eyes open

in the crest of the night,

lying untouched

in my celibate head,

I desired your eyes

as the grey sailed my face,

and silence then spoke

words back from the grave:

You need not water

the withered for those,

whom thought were neglected

to buds have now grown.

Outside this frame

endless passions abound,

but none ring as true

as the sound of your own.

I have telescope eyes
that can only see you,
and a kaleidoscope heart
for all the distorted ways
in which I can love you.

Sometimes we find ourselves
so desperate for an answer,
that we forget to ask the question.
We forget.
That where we need to get,
is not about the actual place,
but about how much we stop
to learn along the way;
that happiness, is not a race.
We forget.
That selling yourself short,
doesn't ever pay.
So we complacently stay,
right here-
wishing we were *there*,
stranded by the fear
that we may take the wrong step
before the right one is revealed.
We forget.
That the fastest way to nowhere
is by standing still.

You will either be
a love professed in ink

or

the messy stain
of spilled apologies.

There is no greater
declaration of
strength
than a woman
who devotedly awaits
the return of a love
she knows she can
never resuscitate.

//The kind of love
everyone kills for
but no one is
willing to die for//

It sickens me to see
how loyalty comes with a
convenience fee sometimes,
how the cost of friendship
is still on the rise and
seldom worth the price.
How unconditional love
was just a convenient
disguise to sell us
fraudulent promises
we were too eager to buy.

Just because we
were meant to
love each other
does not mean
we were meant
to be together.

Some stories
read better
without
the ending.

I have biodegradable
skin that's already
wearing itself thin
under your blistering sun
and an inflatable heart
that will never
keep me afloat
if I ever forget
how to swim back
to the safety of
our sinking boat.

//Capsized//

If you had
truly loved me
for all the
right reasons,
then you
wouldn't have
stopped
for all the
wrong ones.

The most
terrifying
thing in
the world
is to be what
you are not.
Another leader
lost in a sea
of followers,
soon to be forgot.

The air smothered the inexperienced.

The room was poignantly bare, overly avoided.

Dust and lint was sprinkled everywhere

except on a visibly mistreated book

on the far side of the room,

cloaked by the comforting shadows.

The edges of its sheets were flimsy from

constant handling and the ink on the pages

was faded from reading it too much.

This was the accomplice to all her curiosity.

On those desperate nights where there

were more questions than answers,

she would ease the needle into

the pit of her arm and hold her breath

as she drew the coarse blood, momentarily

indulging in the culmination of release-

such an ancient burden quickly put to ease.

With startling precision, she removed

the syringe from her defiled blood and

held it over the attentive surface of the book.

As the weight of the world forced the

corrupted drops onto the pristine slice of paper,

the crimson liquid scattered about the page
and clung to its rightful place,
where the words it formed would
later be read with a heavier heart.
On the opposite side of the room
was a neglected plant.
At its foot lay a pair of worn shoes
which she would soon grow into
and a set of keys which everyone
had forgotten what they opened.

To know that the way to her

heart always needs to be paved,

that she craves to be craved,

to be picked up and read,

to be opened instead of displayed.

I've never

witnessed

a flower

curl up into

itself as

quickly as

I did this

morning,

when you

opened

your eyes

to greet

the world,

and stole

all of

its glory.

My words fit like a glove

around her silence,

eloquently writing

our love

in every language

on the tip of our tongues.

A slip of the tongue

and I come undone,

a physical reaction to

a chemical attraction we

could no longer prolong.

//Chemistry//

When we learn
to use our words
in place of our hands,
we can love people
in places our touch
cannot reach
and our minds
cannot understand.

//Speaking in romance//

I don't want to protect you.
I want to create a world
around you where you will
no longer have any need
for protection.

Today is not a day for words.

I have things to say to you

but my lips refuse

to communicate

the audible way.

Instead, I will convey

the unspeakable

with the eloquence of my kiss.

I will write old-fashioned

love letters upon your doting lips

so they may drink from my ink

and savor every word

your ears have never heard

another lover speak

in the *aphrodisiacal language*

of a starving poet's kiss.

Your bare chest
pressed against
the silhouette
of my back,
all is still black.
Except for the
unmistakable smell
that is you.
The rise and fall
of your breathing
in tandem with mine,
your lips like petals
romancing my ear,
I can't feel you
near enough,
here enough,
take me in,
make me
disappear.

I will find a way to breach

the close-knit fibers of your skin

so I can make my way in

just deep enough

to infiltrate your innermost

thoughts while you sleep.

To leave my fingerprints

on your pericardium walls

so when someone tries to be

heroic with your heart,

they will know from the very start

that my hands have always been

the ones to hold it together

when falling apart.

To rearrange your genes

so that your blood type is *me-*

and you can no longer exist

without my crimson love

flowing through every capillary

of your internal circuitry,

the only way it was always

meant to be.

//Identity Thief//

120

I would wake you up with the softest
kiss right now, so tender and sweet.
And with your eyes still closed, you
could taste that it's me and I could
feel the edges of your mouth curl up
into a smile.

//Good morning//

And for the first time,
none of us knew
what to do with her.
She had me, the sea,
and the moonlit sky
in complete veneration
of her child-like
abandonment.
We were her playground
and she indulged
in every one of us
without restriction.
I couldn't help
but photograph
her every movement,
where she would
forever stay
suspended
in the night.

Her fragile heart
has never been
an open book.
Especially in a world
full of eyes that
don't know where to look.

She still has that admirable
innocence about her that
most of us have long since pawned
in need of a little bit of change,

not knowing we would always remain
a few pennies short of nothing,
in our endless pursuit of everything.

Over time,
I've managed to grow
into this life of mine.
But I fear
that in a few more years
it might fit me too tight
and I might stretch it out
too much
just trying to belong.
So I will wear it in
just long enough
for the wrong to feel
right enough to keep me
moving past the person
I'm conforming to be,
and into the one I was
meant to become all along.
This world is too small
to contain the galaxies
expanding in me.

Sometimes people look at you
and don't *see you.*
They see the outline of you
and cannot yet appreciate what
constitutes your magnificent insides.
But don't get discouraged
or think any less of yourself.
Believe me, you are just as beautiful
as you know yourself to be.
Their eyes have yet to develop fully;
they are still adapting from dark to light,
dilating from black to white.
But give them time
and a little bit of heartbreak,
and their loss will become
conspicuously clear in hindsight.

Don't let the climb intimidate you.
You have empty lungs to fill and
there is always fresher air
the more you go uphill;
you are almost there
just don't.
stand.
still.

In this freeze dried, vacuum packed,
chemically sterilized white room,
nothing dies, they said.
It's designed to preserve instead
all of the tormented minds that come
to write their way back from the dead.
It was the prison cell that would
liberate me from the inside,
reviving me from this catatonic sleep
I woke up in, like a lobotomy
disconnecting me from myself.
It was a glimpse of heaven
from the center of hell, a hope
you could never sell me if I
wasn't so high off these lows.
Funny how an overdose of nothingness
can cure just about anything when
you've had just about enough of it.

//Writer's block//

I can give you the
love of a lifetime,
but only for tonight.

It's nights like tonight
that I can't escape from.
The ones I fill with distractions
to avoid the important questions.
Those where the silence
is so unbearably deafening
that I drink to not think;
I drink to take the sting
out of rejection,
until every last sorrow
sinks to the bottom
of this quickly waning bottle,
and my straightest convictions
are drunk off their own
twisted reflections.
It's been a while since I
recognize my own complexion,
for I've left too many parts of
myself inside all the wrong hearts
with all the right intentions.
I can only feel things
in parts now,

forgive me if I start
to fall apart now
but I need to learn
how to put myself
back together again.
What's left of my love
is too scarce to be shared,
I just hope it's enough
for my hope to be spared.

When we love

in different lights,

the same truth can vary

when seen through a

different set of eyes;

so to rely solely on sight

is to make yourself blind,

and two *distinct truths*

don't always equal a lie.

//The problem with being right//

I tasted the color of your hair

in the smell of my coffee

this morning, and I wondered-

in what *fleeting moment*

did I learn you so well?

When did our cells

become so intertwined?

When did you slip through

the cracks in my shell,

crawl up my spine,

and tuck yourself into

the folds of my mind?

I couldn't tell when you

sought out to strip down

the walls I'd erected so tall,

from the sticks and the stones

that I'd strewn together,

from the brittle old bones

I'd collected from remnants

that past winds had blown

in hopes that one day,

we'd make homes

out of people again.

And although I'm a dreamer by choice,

the realist in me can't pretend

that I have what you need,

and you can't depend on

what you want to believe,

I don't want you to leave

but I won't ask you to wait;

I don't know

if tomorrow's too late

for the two of us.

My level head's in one place

but my riddled heart's in a few,

and all that I knew

was that I couldn't

go through this again.

You see, I know how this ends,

I've been through this before-

fought both sides of this

internal Civil War enough times

to know what's at stake

if we open this door.

My love and affection

are riddled with imperfections.

No matter how good my intentions,

they'll never live up

to your expectations,

our patience will bend,

and bend 'till it breaks

and the biggest mistake

we will make is to believe

we can take whatever it takes

to weather this storm.

I can't be who you need me to be.

I can only show you

the right way to the wrong me

and uncertainty

is the air that we breathe

when the sweetest of means

will never justify the bitter end;

so please understand

why I have to be cruel to be kind.

But if only I'd known that

a storm of *this kind*

has a mind of its own,

that the seedling of feelings

I fought so hard to suppress,

had already been sewn into my

fertile head now ripe with a mess

of conflicting thoughts
as I sit here in waiting,
storm clouds precipitating around me
with the incessant pounding
of a thousand needle pricks
stirring up a commotion inside me
like a restless ocean,
a riptide of emotions
ripping apart every membrane
to let the acid rain in;
my veins, they swell up
with the pressure of going insane
like a high speed train
that was derailed off the
electric rails in my brain
because no one can stop it-
not the brakes, the conductor,
or even the pen that designed it.
Like a spectator to my own tragedy
I was blinded
by the back-breaking fear...
that I'd break you, my dear.
Now I'm choked up on words,
on thoughts misconstrued,

impulsive decisions

I haven't thought through,

intangible doubts

I never outgrew,

the lingering threats

of future regrets,

the imminent mess

of all that I do...

What did I just do?

I never knew that loneliness

can take up so much space

as it rushed in to replace all

the words that I'd left unspoken

with these boisterous echoes of silence...

so sick was this silence

that fondled my hearts strings

like harp strings

to the tune of the blues

in the hues in your eyes

as you folded what's left

of my muse, while wringing it dry

and packed the last drop away

neatly inside the high walls

of your suitcase along with

your socks and our talks, and
that confident way that you walk
when you know you should leave
to spare you the grief
of one last goodbye
in this malleable world we mold
around the holes in our hearts
that have never been whole.
I don't know what *whole* feels like,
because even when blessed by the rain,
the thirst will remain in our souls
simply because, we've tasted before
and acquired a taste
like a favorite whore
to appease this insatiable hunger
that only gets stronger
the longer we plead for its end.
And although my heart
has never known famine,
neither has it feasted
but *at least* its known passion.
So don't ask me to ration my
compliments, my sugarcane kisses
that linger, the way my fingers

retrace the slopes of your breasts

as I slowly undress you, the way

I caress your womanly figure,

eroding your streams,

meandering rivers that lead to

the small of your hips in the form

of a love note I wrote with

my lips on your skin

so you'll always remember

our long conversations,

the seismic vibrations that

stirred up our spirits and

quelled our frustrations,

became our salvation as we floated

on clouds of white sheets and

wished on starlit ceilings

and spilled thoughts about feelings,

and questions of thoughts

we were feeling, and the *meanings*

of these feelings and slowly but surely,

we figured it out;

what our breed's mostly about;

how our excessive need to succeed

brought about all this greed we're about.

Why what we want, is never what we *need*.

Why in the calm of the storm

we complain of a drought;

why our greatest opponent

is our very own doubt in ourselves,

in our worth; but is it all worth

that unopened bottle of whiskey

you saved for that one single problem

unnamed, to drown it all out?

So we pour our drink tall,

to never fall short.

And cheers to the years of

leaving our fears in the past

as soon as we realize at last

that nothing will last in this drought.

As much as I'd like to be yours,

no woman can ever be *woman enough*

for a heart that isn't ready,

for a love that knocks too soon

on a door that is too heavy

to break down with force.

And nothing that's meant to be yours,

should ever be taken with force.

I wonder how
many hearts
have been broken,
by never being
touched...

She's a good person
to love from a distance.
I could watch her forever...
The unrehearsed way
she takes on each day,
the way she wears
the wild in her hair
to match her eyes,
she's art personified.
How she colors everything
caught in the wake of her smile.
How her hips sway, undisturbed
by the weight of her pockets
overflowed at the seams
with dreams too big
for small minds to understand.
At times I'm inclined to let her know
that the majestic way that she flows
is too much for this world to handle.
But I stop myself short,
because I don't want to disturb
a single thing about her.

You can keep your
prophylactic love
and your artificially
sweetened lips.
The type
I'm looking for
is bitter
to the taste,
for it was ground
from the backbones
of hardship and
failed attempts
to never let it
go to waste.

//Don't soften the blow for me//

Some days
should be framed
and hung up on display;
the way the sky's rays
play with your hair
and the trees sway with
every breath you exhale
in an artistic affair
between creator and muse.
You are the fuse for
every fire your matchstick
lips have flared.
With eyes like those of
a wild beast on the prowl,
you howl at the dark side
of the moon, asking her
to extend her glowing arms
for the two of you to
reunite again soon.

Find people that are
multidimensional. Ones
that will contribute to
your existence instead of
complicate it. Ones that will
foster your individuality
instead of criticize it. Ones
that will not pass judgement
on an original thought
simply because they don't yet
understand it. Find people
you can grow with while
everyone else continues to
worry too much about why
they can't stop you.

I don't
purposely
romanticize
everything,
it's just how
I see the
world. . .

My dear, you don't have to choose.
You're a lover, a fighter, a poet and a muse.

But to think you should settle for one or the other,
for what is a lover without the heart of a fighter
or a writer without her loving muse?

In those times when you hurt

every which way you turn,

it is hard not to be selfish.

To not want to reach out

for the first person to offer

any amount of distraction,

even the slightest relief.

And damned if you need it,

you're being shaken at the core.

But those are also the times

your character is being forged.

Remember that the arms you use

to recreate that feeling of

belonging, don't belong to you.

That in a moment of weakness,

you have enough strength

to break someone else.

Don't bring others down

with your sadness,

it is for only you to feel.

Because when it is done with you,

you will have learned

to love it too;

for even then,

it filled up that emptiness in you.

//When we break up we break down//

Your motivation

to get ahead

should be

your refusal

to be left behind.

I've run out of ways
to try to cheat myself
out of loving you.
I almost got away
with it once, nearly
eradicating the memory of you
from my thoughts completely;
Except it wasn't the thought of you
that made me miss you this time,
but the absence of it
that never felt quite right.

Perhaps my
greatest mistake
is that I always
expected
way too much
of friends,
and not enough
of lovers.

People say I give too much of
myself sometimes. They say I
should value more of my time,
ration my feelings and reserve
my love for the few that prove
themselves worthy of it. But
the truth is, I do it for them
as much as I do it for myself;
for I have so much love to give
that it overflows out of me in
every direction. Whether they
deserve it or not, it is not
for me to decide. There is always
the slight chance that they may
need it, and that makes all the
difference in the world to me,
if I can make a world of a
difference to them.

//I didn't know what to do with
so much love, so I gave it to you//

The

emptier

the

heart,

the

heavier

it

is

to

carry.

Hours of tedious effort
were required to write
that riveting "one true sentence"
that seemed so damn simple
when read.
Writing was demanding,
solitary, back-breaking work.
A writer mines the tunnels
of their mind using words
as their pickaxe.
A week's efforts may yield
only one nugget worth keeping,
and you could weep with
pathetic gratitude over that.

//The process//

You're going back again?
That's just the extent
of how *lost* you really are.
Don't confuse it
for you being *found*.

Don't ever get stuck
being the only one
on your knees
trying to piece things
back together again.
Anything worth fixing
will never fall apart
so easily.
If it does, that means
it was fragile
from the very start.

Anyone that tells you
they may eventually
let you down,
does not want you
to prove them wrong.
It doesn't matter
how many times
they've let people
down in the past,
patterns are just excuses.
If they ever truly imagined
the possibility
of a future with you,
they would have also imagined
none *without* you.

Be conservative with your curiosity.

Remember we offer our identity

as collateral every time

we set out to find ourselves.

//We are the sum of our experiences//

There's a light that radiates
from inside of you that
everyone is drawn to
like moths, in awe
of its brilliance yet none
have the slightest clue
what to do with it all,
for you are not one, but
a *constellation of stars*
in a city of broken lights.

She keeps
getting called
further away
from everything
she's ever known.

and closer to *home.*

I'm coming back
for you, my dear.
Know that I never left.
I just went to go shed
the parts of me that
should have been dead
a long time ago.
I've been learning to let go
of my reluctance to hold on
to a good thing for too long;
of the illegitimate fears
that have managed to steal
the air from my lungs,
the life from my years and
the words from my tongue.
I'll admit I was wrong for
allowing myself to stray so far
beyond my own recognition;
it's the symptomatic part of
this latent human condition
I have yet to fully tame.

I guess I thought I could spare
myself the inevitable pain
of falling apart if we were never
really put together from the start.

Believe me,
I've been working on myself;
making more room *inside* myself
to allow me grow back into
the woman I used to be,
instead of the traces of her
that were left, by the time
you first laid eyes on me.
It's never too late when
it's well worth the wait.
I'm coming back
for you, my dear.

//I'm writing my wrongs,
I'm fixing my love for you//

I know I have your heart on a loan
but I've grown quite fond of the home
it's made together with mine.
If you would allow me inside,
I would decorate its walls
with every fallen star that
has ever gone unwished upon
in hopes that with time,
I could finally come to call it my own.

I was never one for
optimistic story lines
that flow like poetry
off the tongue.
For sticking around
after our time was done,
for believing
in happy endings
from sad beginnings
or recognizing love
while I'm still in it.
But in my own defense,
I also never knew you existed.

This paper
heart is torn
between following
you out to sea,
and seeking refuge
from your storm.

Her skin was made of night,
thinly sliced and draped to hide
the galaxies asleep
deep inside her bones.
She had eyes like libraries
full of wisdom centuries old
and a smile warm like a fireplace
to keep away the underlying cold.
Her arms felt like promises
backed by solid gold,
for they never fail to add worth
to those they hold close.
She was a wandering soul
and I was the home
she walked into this time,
the inviting bed where
she would lay her weary head
to rest on my beating chest,
hands curled into mine,
jointly traces the fall of the stars
and orchestrating the skies
to do pirouettes *just for us,*
against the silhouette of the night.

If
we
can't
grow
together,

we
must
grow
apart.

Cover me in kerosene

and ignite the darkest

depths of me. Set ablaze

these wick-like veins

and let the hungry flames

devour the lonely hours

that swallow me. I know

just how hard it can be

to let light in when people

keep taking it with them

whenever they leave; but

sometimes, we'll come to find

that the most beautiful parts

of ourselves are hidden in places

where that light cannot reach

and the darkness feels good

against our paling skin.

So hold on tight

to the promise of night,

for everyone knows

the slow death of a star

is what keeps it alive.

Am I breaking
or am I healing?
I could never
quite define
these feelings
that I'm feeling.

I wanted you
to look at me
the way I
look at her
so you can feel
your soul break
under the
crushing weight
of the things
that should
have been
but never
were.

I am a bird
who's taken the time
to grow out its wings-
solely to rip through
the fault lines of
this converging sky
where you and I
can violently collide
into fireworks,
only to discover
my newborn fear of heights.

It's not the rise
that intimidates me,
it's not knowing how far
I can go with my wings
before they betray me;
It's the unnerving fall,
the suspense of making sense
of it all when the more I have,
the more I have to *lose*.

//Learning to rise with the fall//

I've walked into people's lives
before where I've had to make
myself smaller in order to fit
into it. Alternately, people have
walked into mine where there has
been so much space left over, their
presence is barely noticeable.

//Spatial Intelligence//

At some point in your life,
you will come across someone
for the very first time that
you will have some unfinished
business with. You will come to
find that their hand fits so
perfectly in yours, because you
have been holding on to each other
for many lifetimes now without ever
letting go. What a magical thing
that must be, to *just know* that on
any given day, in any given town,
across some busy street, your eyes
will finally come to meet, and your
souls will reunite.

//You've lived many lives before,
I can wait for one more//

Your scent smells like coming home...

She was a fragile masterpiece.
I felt I could break her simply by admiring her beauty for too long.

My
favorite
kiss
was
the
one
you
couldn't
give.

I like how well
I fit into you.
I like how your lips
always know what to do
and the way my fingertips
are always missing you...